Go Wild

BE A SURVIVOR

By Chris Oxlade

Illustrated by Eva Sassin

HUNGRY
TOMATO™

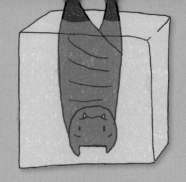

CONTENTS

TIME TO GO WILD

Where do you go to have fun? Have you discovered the great outdoors? No? Then it's time to go wild! Go exploring, see amazing natural sights, have loads of fun and learn how to survive outside! So how about putting down your tablet, switching off your games console, stepping out of the door and trying some of the great activities in this book. Even if you live in the middle of the city, you can have a wild time in your garden or your local park.

In Go Wild — Be a Survivor, discover some of the skills you'll need to survive in the wild: building camps, lighting fires, getting water and signalling for help if you need to.

WILD SAFETY

• Never go exploring in the wild without an adult.

• Ask an adult before you do any of the projects in this book. In particular, ask before going near or in water, going to the coast, exploring in bad weather or in the dark, and using a GPS.

CARING FOR THE ENVIRONMENT

Always take care of the environment when you are in the wild. That means:

• Never damage rocks, animals or plants.

• Take special care to keep fires under control, and make sure a fire is out before you leave it.

SURVIVAL STUFF

THE KIT YOU NEED TO SURVIVE

You never know exactly what nature will throw at you when you head out into the wild! So it's wise to have a survival kit in your rucksack. You can use your kit for some of the projects later in the book.

Put together a survival kit

Here are all the bits and pieces you will need.

A simple first-aid kit containing a few sticking plasters, a bandage and some safety pins

A small metal tin or plastic box to store your survival kit

A small mirror

A whistle

A few metres of para cord (a strong, artificial cord)

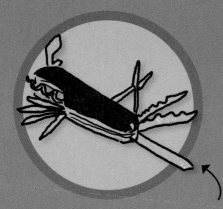

A penknife or multi-tool. Ask an adult before you use this

A pencil and a few small sheets of paper

A fire steel and flint, for lighting a fire

An emergency thermal blanket to keep you warm if you need to wait for help

Some waterproof matches

Some emergency food, such as snack bars

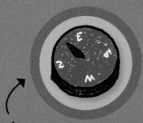

A button compass

A torch

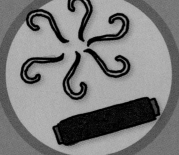

A few metres of fishing line and some small fishing hooks

FIGHTING FEAR

If you can stay calm when others are panicking, you have a better chance of survival! So try to:

• keep cool and collected if you can

• make the right decisions at all times – for example, never cross a raging river

• prepare for the worst but hope for the best!

• never give up!

TAKE COVER!

Spider tent

BUILDING A SHELTER

The weather can be a terrible foe in the wild. Wind and rain make you chilly and damp, and strong sunshine can fry you to a crisp. Luckily, it's not too tricky to craft a shelter that'll keep the elements (oh, and some wild beasts) at bay.

Argh! Bear!

A lean-to shelter

The simplest of all ...

1. Find a tree with a branch sticking out about 1 metre above the ground.

2. Find a branch about 2.5 metres long. Rest one end in the V between the tree trunk and the branch to make a top beam for your shelter.

WHERE TO BUILD?

You can build your shelter pretty much anywhere, but steer clear of places like hilltops, where you could be blown away, or right next to streams or in hollows, where you could be flooded out.

3. Lean plenty of branches at an angle from the ground against the beam on both sides.

4. Smother the branches in dead leaves or more leafy branches.

5. Throw more dry leaves on the ground to make your shelter more comfy.

6. Snuggle inside, feet first.

An A-frame

Can't find a tree to support your shelter? Use this handy frame instead, or use two frames to support a tent-shaped shelter.

1. Tie the end of a piece of paracord to a 1.5-metre-long stick, about 25 centimetres from one end, with a clove hitch as shown above.

2. Put another stick next to the first one.

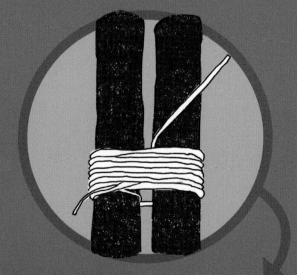

3. Wrap the cord around both sticks about 10 times, but not too tightly.

4. Wrap the cord around the turns of rope between the two sticks — twice, and tightly.

5. Tie the end of the rope around the second stick, again with a clove hitch.

6. That's it! Pull the ends of the sticks apart to form your A-frame.

Always ask permission before tying up a friend!

9

ICY IGLOOS

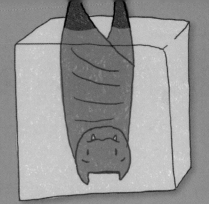

BUILDING SNOW SHELTERS

When it snows in the wild, you can build a simple windbreak or even an igloo using the snow itself. It might be hard work, and take you a few hours, but it'll be worth the effort. Igloos are traditional temporary shelters built by Inuit people in the Arctic.

Building a snow windbreak

1. Make a snow block by packing snow into a plastic box and stamping it firmly down.

2. Lay blocks end-to-end to make a low curved wall, with the outside of the wall towards the wind.

3. Add a second layer of blocks to make the wall higher. Keep adding layers until the wall is high enough to crouch behind. Stuff snow into any gaps.

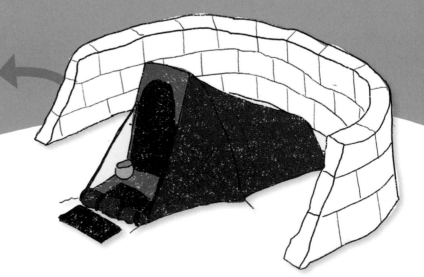

Making an igloo shelter

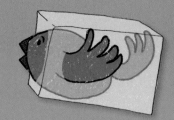

IGLOO SAFETY

Don't make the igloo too big – ice blocks can be heavy and you don't want them to trap you if it collapses!

1. Mark out a circle in the snow about 1 metre across.

2. Make snow blocks (see step 1 left), and build a snow wall around the circle, leaving a gap for a door. You could start with the snow wall you built before.

3. Add more blocks to make another layer of your wall, but place the blocks at a slight angle so the wall leans in slightly.

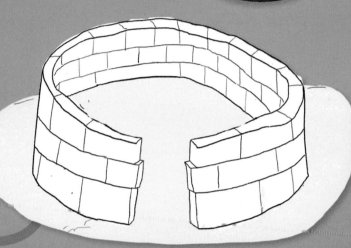

4. Once you've arranged about four or five layers of blocks, you'll need an assistant to support the blocks as you put them in place.

5. Add a capping block to fill the hole in the roof of your igloo, and then stuff snow into any gaps.

6. You can improve your igloo by adding a tunnel at the entrance.

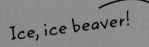

Ice, ice beaver!

WILD WARMTH

MAKING A FIRE

Fire is a lifesaver in the wild. It keeps you warm when it's cold, cooks food, lights up the dark and wards off wild animals. To start a fire you need fuel, heat and air.

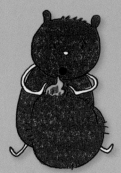

Don't catch your tail on the fire!

FIRE SAFETY

You must always ask an adult before lighting a fire, whether it's in your garden or in the wild. Don't light fires when the weather has been very dry, and don't make your fire so large that it could get out of control.

Lighting a fire

1. Choose a site for your fire, well away from trees. Clear the ground and cut away turf so you can put it back later.

2. Gather tinder, kindling and fuel (see panel).

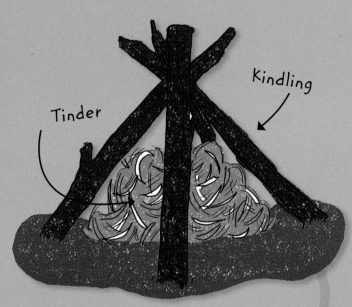

Tinder

Kindling

4. Light the tinder with a match. As the tinder begins to burn, add more tinder, then add kindling.

5. Look after your fire, feeding it with fuel all the time.

3. Lay a mat of dry, dead wood, then arrange your kindling into a small tepee, with the tinder underneath.

6. Always make sure your fire is out and the ashes are cold before you leave. Clear the site and replace turf if you have cut it.

Making a feather stick

Use a feather stick if you can't find any small kindling to get your fire going.

1. Find a dry stick about 1 centimetre thick and use your knife to cut slivers of wood along the sides, so the stick looks feathery.

2. Make a few feather sticks, and keep them ready in case you want to light a fire in a hurry.

BE SAFE

Read page 16 for knife safety tips before you start.

Tinder

FIRE FUEL

To get a fire going, you need:

Tinder — fluffy material that burns very easily, such as dry grass

Kindling — small twigs and other pieces of wood

Fuel — sticks and logs

It's nice to share your fire with friends.

Fire without matches

What happens if you drop your matches in a pond? Don't despair — you can still light a fire without them!

You won't find one if these in the wild!

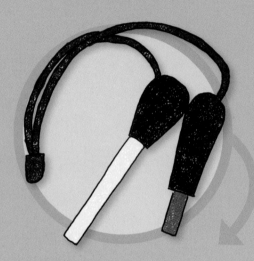

1. A flint and steel is made up of a strip of magnesium metal and a steel striker.

2. To light tinder with a flint and steel, aim the flint at the tinder, press the steel onto it and push the steel down to make a spark. Keep trying until the tinder lights.

3. Once your tinder is smouldering, blow gently to make it burst into flames. Now you can put kindling over the tinder and get your fire going.

4. On a hot, sunny day, you can light a fire with a magnifying glass. Focus the Sun's rays onto tinder until it smoulders, then blow on the tinder as before.

Fire by friction

This fire-lighting method was invented thousands of years ago. It's tricky to make it work, but have a go!

Fire drill

1. Make a fire drill from a straight stick about 50 centimetres long. Sharpen one end and make the other end rounded.

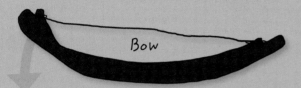
Bow

2. Make a bow from a curved branch and paracord or strong string. The string should be taut, but not too tight.

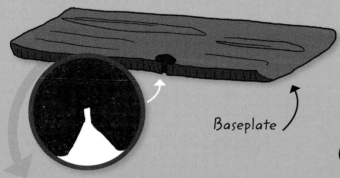
Baseplate

3. Cut a triangular notch about 2 centimetres deep into the side of a wooden baseplate.

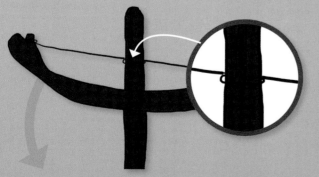

4. Wrap the string of your bow once around your drill. Place the sharp end of the drill into the notch on the baseplate.

socket

5. Press down on top of the stick with a concave stone (one with a small hollow).

6. Ready to make fire? Move the bow backwards and forwards quickly. After a while, you should get black powder in the notch and a scorched hole in the wood.

7. Gradually move the bow faster and faster until the drill begins to smoke. Go faster still, and you should produce a glowing ember in the pile of powder.

8. Transfer the ember to a heap of kindling and blow gently to make flames.

FOR THE CHOP

USING A KNIFE

In the wild you often need to make stuff from the bits of wood you find around you. So you need a knife and the skills to use it properly.

Pen knife

Sheath knife

KNIFE SAFETY

Always ask an adult before using a knife, and make sure you know the local laws about carrying knives. Always keep knives folded up or sheathed when not in use.

Using a penknife safely

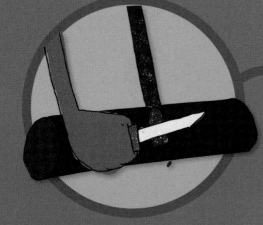

1. Here's how to hold a knife safely. This forehand grip allows you to push down firmly on the knife to make a cut.

2. To make a cut in a stick, first sit down on the ground. Keep the knife and the stick in front of your knees all the time, and cut away from your body. Remember to fold up or sheath the knife afterwards.

3. To make deeper cuts, or cut harder wood, rest the stick on a tree trunk or large log. The same rule applies — always cut away from your body.

Making a walking stick

So heavy!

1. Find a branch about 2 centimetres thick and about 1.5 metres long. Ask an adult to saw off the ends if you can only find a longer branch.

3. Make similar cuts at the other end of the branch, but this time to form a blunt end.

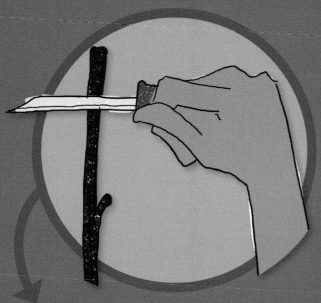

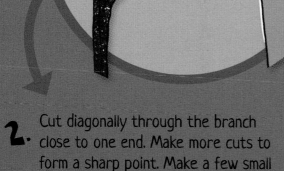

2. Cut diagonally through the branch close to one end. Make more cuts to form a sharp point. Make a few small cuts rather than one or two big ones.

4. Decorate your stick by cutting notches along the sides. To make a notch, rest your stick on a tree trunk or log, make a shallow cut at angle, then angle the blade the other way and make another cut. Remove the waste wood.

Walking sticks aren't very helpful when you're a bird!

Left! Left! Left, Right, Left!

THIRSTY WORK

FINDING WATER

You can't survive without water. So if you're in the wild gasping for a drink but there isn't a river or stream close by, you need to know how to find water.

WATER SAFETY

Never drink water you've found in the wild without sterilizing it first (with special tablets or by boiling it). Never drink salt water. And never drink your own wee.

Water from leaves

You can capture the water that is always evaporating from the leaves of plants.

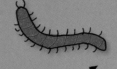

Remember to remove bugs before you sterilize your water!

1. Carefully put a clear plastic bag over the end of a branch of a tree or shrub. Close the neck of the bag and tie it loosely with string.

2. Wait for a few hours, then examine the bag. You should find water has collected in the bottom.

Water from grass

Collect dew from the grass in the early morning by tying towels to your legs and walking around. Then simply squeeze the water from the towels.

18

Water from the Sun

That's not water from the Sun itself, but getting water using the Sun's energy!

1. Find a sunny spot, and dig a shallow pit, about 30 centimetres deep in the ground. Place a dish or other container in the centre of the pit.

2. Put some fresh leaves in and cover the pit with a plastic sheet. Put stones around the edge to hold the plastic sheet in place, and put a small stone in the centre of the sheet to make it sag slightly in the centre.

3. Wait a few hours! Then have a look in the container. Have you got any water?

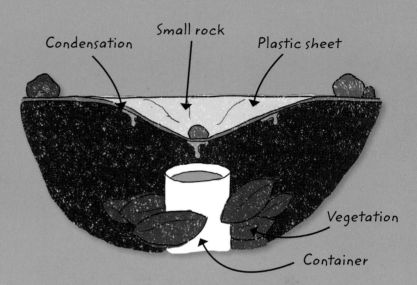

Condensation — Small rock — Plastic sheet

Vegetation

Container

Water from a frog

In a dire emergency you can get water from a frog's body. Only try this under expert supervision! And only in a dire emergency!

1. First you have to find the right sort of frog, such as the water-holding frog that lives in Western Australia! This normally means digging into the ground.

2. Simply squeeze the frog gently sideways, and be ready to catch the water in a dish or in your mouth!

Collecting rainwater

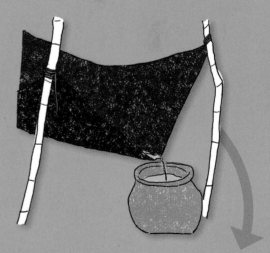

Tie the corners of a plastic sheet to the branches of a tree, with one end of the sheet lower than the other. If it rains, water will pour off the sheet. Catch it in a container.

CATCHING A FEAST

HUNTING AND FISHING

So you've built a shelter, found some water and got your fire going. All you need now is something to eat! Please don't catch any animals to eat unless it's a real survival situation.

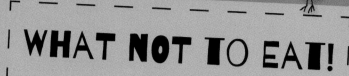

Don't eat us! We are poisonous!

Make a bottle fish trap

2. Reverse the top and push it into the bottle.

1. Cut the top off a plastic pop bottle.

3. Put some bait, such as food scraps, into the bottle.

4. Place your trap underwater for a few hours. Look inside. Any fish?

20

Make a slingshot

Here's a tool you could use for hunting in a survival situation. Never fire it at a person or animal — always at a safe target.

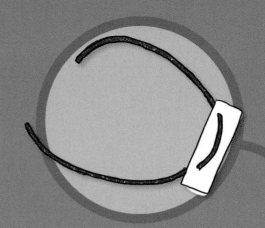

1. Find a tree branch with a neat Y shape, like this one. The wood should be at least 1 centimetre thick.

2. With a knife or saw, cut away the ends to make a Y-shaped piece of wood, about 20 centimetres long.

3. Cut a shallow notch about 2 centimetres from the end of each arm.

4. Prepare a piece of nylon webbing, or a leather strip, about 12 centimetres long. Cut a hole about 2 centimetres from each end.

5. Now you need a length of thick elastic or rubber tubing, about 60 centimetres long. Thread this through the holes in the webbing.

6. Tie the ends of the elastic around the top of the arms of the Y shape, in line with notches.

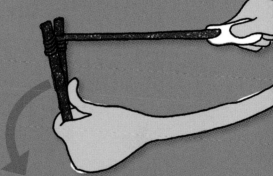

7. To fire your slingshot, put a small stone in the centre of the webbing, grip the stone through the webbing from behind, pull back the webbing, take aim ... and fire!

This might be a bit more than he bargained for!

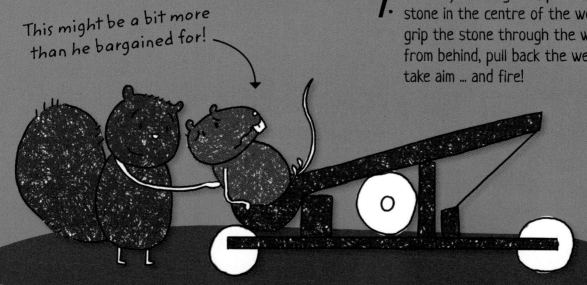

Making a fishing rod

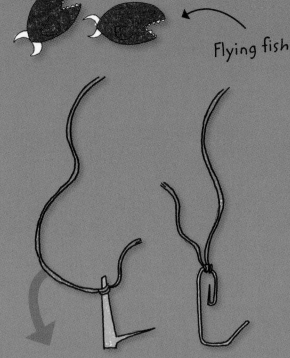

Flying fish

1. Look for a bendy stick at least 2 metres long. A thin, freshly cut bamboo pole is perfect. Cut a small notch close to the thinner end.

2. Tie a length of string about 2 metres long to the thin end of the stick where you cut the notch.

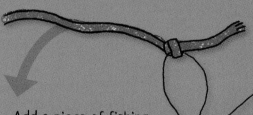

3. Add a piece of fishing line about 2 metres long to the end of the string. To join the string and line, double over the end of the line and tie a loop, then tie the string to the loop.

4. Now tie a fishing hook to the line with a half blood knot, as shown.

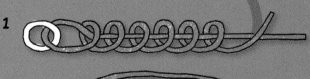

1

2

3

5. If you don't have a fishing hook or line, don't despair! You can make hooks from paper clips and even the thorns from prickly plants such as hawthorn.

6. You can also try fishing with any sort of cord, such as string, cotton, wool and even your shoe laces.

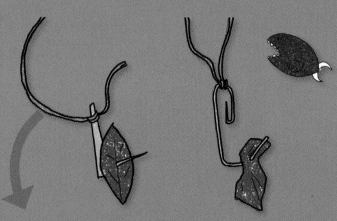

7. For bait you can use food scraps or objects that look like a small fish underwater.

8. Drop your hook and bait into the water. Now wait patiently. If your line wiggles, pull up sharply on the fishing rod to hook the fish.

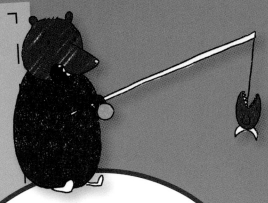

IF YOU **CATCH** A **FISH...**

Don't panic! Wet your hands and hold the fish firmly but not tightly. Carefully remove the hook from the fish's mouth, then return the fish to the water. Always release fish that you don't need for survival.

Spit fishing

1. Stand in the water, and spit into the water in front of you.

2. Wait with your t-shirt ready to scoop up fish attracted to the spit. Simple!

FISHING, SAFETY AND THE LAW

Never go fishing without an adult, and never fish where there is a chance of falling into deep, cold or fast-flowing water. Also be careful of sharp hooks. You should use barbless hooks, which are easier to get out of fish and fingers than barbed ones. Make sure you know the law about fishing — in many places you need a licence to fish.

Fishing by hand

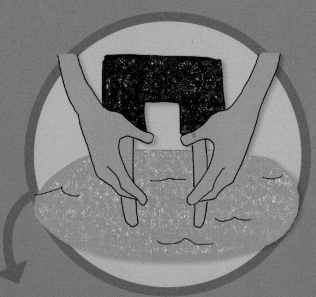

1. Stand very still in shallow water, up to 30 centimetres deep, with your hands cupped.

2. Wait for a fish to come close, then very, very slowly, move your hands around it, and grab it!

WILD FARE

FORAGING FOR FOOD

Plants are on the menu in the wild, as well as fish and other animals. And catching plants is much easier than catching animals! Check out some of the yummy berries, nuts and leaves you can eat.

FORAGING SAFETY

Never eat any part of a plant unless an adult tells you it is safe to do so. Most plants are safe to eat, but there are plenty that you must avoid because they are poisonous. Mushrooms and toadstools can be especially dangerous. Only collect them with the help of an expert.

Collecting berries and nuts

Nuts and berries are a good source of energy.

1. Blackberries, bilberries and cranberries are all edible. You can eat them raw or stew them in a pot over your camp fire.

2. Search for nuts, such as hazelnuts and sweet chestnuts, which you can eat raw. Collect acorns, too, but boil them a few times in water to stop them tasting bitter.

Bilberries

Blackberries

Cranberries

Hazelnuts

Acorns

Sweet chestnuts

Sssssss-so tasty!

Collecting leaves

Eating leaves might not seem ideal, but many herbs are leaves, and so are salad ingredients. You can find similar leaves to eat in the wild.

Dandelion →

1. Search for dandelion, sorrel and stinging nettle leaves. You can also eat watercress if you find it near rivers.

Sorrel →

Stinging nettle →

2. You can make delicious tea from stinging nettles. Pick the leaves of young plants, wearing gloves to avoid being stung. Wash the leaves with fresh water.

3. Put the leaves in a pan of boiling water and boil them for a few minutes, until the water looks slightly green. Allow the water to cool a little before drinking. Don't worry, the nettles can't sting any more!

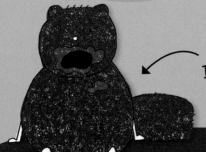
I shouldn't have eaten ALL the blackberries!

Don't eat me! I am purple, but I am not a blackberry!

FOOD ON FIRE

COOKING OVER A CAMP FIRE

If you've found some food to eat in the wild, you can make a fire (see page 12) and cook the food over it. To practise cooking over a fire, try these projects with food from home.

Making a pot support

Here's how to suspend a kettle over a fire for heating and purifying water in a pot.

1. Find a stick or branch with a fork in it. Shorten the ends to make a stick with a forked end, about 50 centimetres long. Sharpen the single end.

2. Push the stick into the ground close to your fire, but not so close that it will burn.

3. Find a stick about 1.5 metres long. Cut off the side branches, then cut a deep notch about 2 centimetres from the thin end of the stick.

4. Place the long stick in the support, so that one end rests on the ground and the other end is over the fire, high enough up so that it doesn't burn. Use a log or large stone to hold the stick steady.

Now you can make some nettle tea (see page 25)!

5. Hang your kettle in the notch, being careful of the fire.

Cooking in foil

Use this method for cooking potatoes and other vegetables in your fire.

1. Wrap your potatoes, parsnips or bits of swede in foil and drop them in the centre of the fire. Keep your hands away from the flames.

2. Give the vegetables half an hour to cook. Use a stick to roll them out of the fire, then ask an adult to unwrap them.

Making a skewer

Any food that you can put on a skewer can be cooked over your fire. That includes marshmallows, sausages and vegetables.

1. Make a pot support as before.

2. Find thin, green sticks and shave off the bark to make skewers.

Even when cooked, worms will probably be icky!

3. Attach a skewer to a longer stick by wrapping string around both. Push your food onto the skewer and rest the stick in the support so that the food is over the fire.

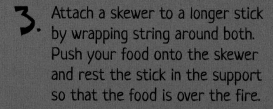

I'm a survival chef!

SOS!

Don't light your fire until you are ready!

CALLING FOR HELP

If you're trapped in the wild, you need to know how to call for help. Remember that there probably won't be a mobile phone signal where you are. Or you might have dropped your phone in a river! Never call for help unless there is a real emergency.

Fire signals

Bright flames will attract rescuers at night, and smoke will attract rescuers in the day. Light your rescue fire in a clearing on a hilltop.

1. First, gather up all the fuel you need for a fire, and build a fire so that it is ready to light (see page 12).

2. Keep a look out. Only light your fire when help is in sight. In the day, make smoke by putting branches with green leaves over the fire.

3. Remember to put the fire out after you have been rescued.

Make a heliograph

You can use a mirror, which you should have in your survival kit, to signal, using light from the Sun. This is called a heliograph.

1. Hold the heliograph so that it bounces sunlight towards the ground (you can also use a metal tin or pair of glasses to reflect from the Sun). Practise moving the spot by tilting the heliograph left or right, and up or down.

2. To send an SOS, signal an aircraft with three short flashes, three long flashes, and three short flashes again.

GROUND-TO AIR-SIGNALS

These internationally agreed signals will work anywhere in the world!

I = Serious injury

F = Need food and water

A = Yes

N = No

X = Unable to move

→ = Moving this way

LL = All is well

Ground signals

Make shapes on the ground that can be seen from the air.

1. Find a large open space that can be seen from the air.

2. Make a signal as large as possible using branches, by clearing leaves or tramping hollows in snow.

Serious injury

Need food and water

Yes

No

Unable to move

Moving this way

All is well

DID YOU KNOW?

○ Humans discovered how to light fires at least a million years ago. Traces of fires this old have been found in a cave in South Africa.

○ You can make fire from ice! Simply find a slab of very clear ice, shape it into a convex lens, and use it to focus sunlight onto tinder.

○ You can also make fire using an empty drink's can. Use the dish-shaped base to focus sunlight onto tinder.

○ Have you heard of the fire triangle? It's made up of the three things you need to get a fire going: fuel, oxygen (from the air) and heat.

○ Around 15,000 years ago humans who lived by hunting and gathering in Europe made dome-shaped shelters from the huge bones of mammoths.

○ The largest igloo ever built was made by an adventure sports company in Canada in 2011. It measured 9.3 metres (30 feet 6 inches) across, and contained 2,500 blocks of snow.

○ In 2003 Aron Ralston was exploring a canyon in Utah, USA, when a massive boulder fell and trapped his arm. After few days, he realized the only way to survive was to cut off his arm with his outdoor knife. The movie *127 Hours* is based on his terrible experience.

○ British mountaineer Joe Simpson was climbing in the Andes when he fell and broke his leg. He later slipped into a crevasse. He was in terrible pain, had no food or water, but he crawled back to safety. It took him four days.

○ Scotsman Alexander Selkirk was left alone on a Pacific island in 1704. He survived there for four and a half years before being rescued. The story of Robinson Crusoe is based on Selkirk's adventure.

○ You need to drink 2 litres (4 pints) of water a day to stay healthy. That's about eight full glasses. You should drink more when the weather's hot or when you're doing strenuous exercise.

○ People have survived without water by drinking their own wee. But it's a last resort – never try it!

○ The slingshot, or catapult, became a popular toy after inflatable tyres were invented in 1888. Children used old inner tubes for slingshot elastic.

○ The rosary pea, native to India, is the most poisonous plant that exists. The plant's red and black seeds contain a deadly chemical.

○ In 1894 soldiers of the US Army sent a message between two hilltops 295 kilometres (183 miles) apart, using mirrors to reflect the Sun.

Oh no!
Not again!

INDEX

THE AUTHOR
Chris Oxlade is an experienced author of educational books for children. He has written more than two hundred books on science, technology, sports and hobbies, including many activity and project books. He enjoys camping and adventurous outdoor sports including rock climbing, hill running, kayaking and sailing. He lives in England with his wife, children, and dogs.

THE ARTIST
Eva Sassin is a freelance illustrator born and bred in London. She has loved illustrating ever since she can remember, and she loves combining characters with unusual textures to give them more depth and keep them interesting.